CLIENT BAIT

*How To Use Content Marketing
To Add Value, Build Trust
And Get New Clients*

JEREMY JONES

Legal Disclaimer

CONTENTS

"If you have any questions, tweet me @jonesima with #ClientBait"
-Jeremy, AskJeremyJones.com

Gain access to free exclusive book bonus training on how to gain massive exposure of your content marketing in as little as 15 minutes per day. On your cell phone text CLIENTBAIT to phone number 33444

Jeremy's Recommendations:

"Jeremy is a great personal and professional coach. I saw him first hand as he mentored someone who was passionate about getting into business and the insights and information he imparted was some of the highest quality I have ever seen. Its like getting years of Business School training packed into a few sessions. With Jeremy's help, it won't be a question of if you succeed, it will just be a matter of when. " -Brian Culhane, eXp Realty

"Within a few minutes of a coaching sessions with Jeremy Jones, I rediscovered hope. I consulted with him about a situation that was spiraling out of control and through his guidance I was able to figure out a usable action plan. I'm now implementing that plan and I'm excited to reclaim some freedom!" -Kimanzi Constable   Author, International Speaker, Consultant

Jeremy has been a great adviser and educator along the path to achieving my goals. Friendly, helpful, and unassuming he gently guides clients to their potential by offering rock solid advice and a framework for productive action. His approach is similar to a counselor – encouraging and motivational. Jeremy is also creative and skilled enough to complete critical tasks (or point you in the direction of excellent resources) that help build your business. Even if you never meet face-to-face, you will feel that the person on the other end of the phone has your best interests at heart. I would recommend Jeremy to anyone seeking marketing coaching. His services are unmatched and it's been a pleasure working with him. -Tiffany Lardomita, founder at Inner View Studios

ACKNOWLEDGEMENTS

Special Thanks to those that have helped to give me a real appreciation for value based marketing. Bob Burg has helped me with a Go-Giver attitude and my first real referral marketing education through his books and programs and now proud to call a friend. Bill Heitzman for your friendship, mentorship and guidance with the Leadership Productivity Forum. Joe Polish for inviting me to contribute to your team and creating such great marketing education through the ILoveMarketing.com Podcast. Kevin Thompson for showing me how to sincerely appreciate people and create a win-win JV relationship. Mike Koenigs for your great example of being filled with joy and life, being a great dad and teaching people to be a creator, not just a consumer. Dan Kuschell for always offering advice and help on marketing and influence. Steve Fischman for your example of long term consistency. Larry Beacham for your coaching and support on marketing.

Tom Challan for your coaching on connecting with people and building friendships. Jordan Adler for your steady work ethic and how you showed me the power of keeping things simple to grow exponentially. Jodi Low for creating and awesome community I'm a part of with U & Improved. To many more authors, friends, entrepreneurs and coaches that have invested time to take years of wisdom, insights and ideas to put them into books, coaching and programs to help people get the same results or better than you, in less time. Most importantly I'm humbled by God's grace, unconditional

Jeremy Jones

love and favor in my life, and special thanks to the most important person in my life that has stood by me in the good times and bad times, and who always believed in me even when I didn't believe in myself at times, the love of my life, my wife Claudia. Finally, I want to thank the incredible team at Jones Media Publishing who help contribute to this project.

- 6 -

INTRODUCTION

W HEN YOU COMPLETE this book you'll find that it will serve as a resource and guide for any small business owner, freelancer or entrepreneur who would like to leverage content marketing, leverage your time on social media and get new customers. Content Marketing is a term to describe putting out content such as audio, video or written as a way to attract a customer based on a topic they are interested in.

This can also serve as a guide to start making money with your blog if you don't have a product yet or you're starting a business online for the first time and would like to do it with a blog.

This guide will will both highlight the importance of blogging, and explain to you why you may be wasting time trying to market by "branding" rather than using direct response marketing to get clients and letting the branding happen as a result of your outreach.

My goal with this guide is to give you a blueprint of how you can use a blog whether you have a product or service to offer now or not and develop a profitable online business or leverage your marketing efforts with an existing business.

You will learn here a very simple 3 step process that anyone could follow by using a blog online and offline. I chose to use Twitter as the social platform because I believe it's the best way to leverage your marketing online and get new readers and subscribers quickly, but these ideas can apply to whatever social network you prefer.

What you need to know

This guide will not explain to you how to set up a blog. Some of the terms I'll be using will be in regards to using a Wordpress blog only because it's the blog platform I use and it's one of the most common used. In the section on sharing and syndicating your blog I talk about "social sharing" buttons, this assumes you have a plugin selected you prefer in added social sharing with all the social networks you prefer to list.

When you add social sharing buttons to each blog post you won't be visiting each social network to share your blog, you can share it out directly from the post and you make it easy for the reader to share your content. Lastly, you will benefit most from this book if you have a blog already in place and are not quite sure how to use it effectively.

You can use Wordpress.com or Tumblr to set up a free blog that doesn't require hosting, however I recommend you have a website and own the hosting account where your blog is hosted.

Our conversation here about blogging with have some common terms if you are familiar with using a Wordpress blog, if there are any terms you don't understand you can most likely find them by searching on Wordpress help sites.

CHAPTER 1

The Online Branding Rat Race

MOST PEOPLE WHO try to promote their business on social media are doing it wrong. If you ask them why they try to promote their business on Facebook or Twitter, they'll say they're trying to "build their brand" or "get exposure" or – the most popular answer – "to get my name out there."

Does it work? Sure, it works in some random cases. Is it the most effective way to do promotion? No.

Early in 2014 I went to see my friend Gary Vaynerchuk, who wrote The Thank You Economy and his first book, Crush It. It was at a book signing in Tempe, Arizona. I've had Gary as a guest on my podcast two times. He's a very driven guy and well known as a savvy social-media entrepreneur.

At this book signing I ran into Joe Polish, who I've known from local events. I was a regular listener to his popular podcast, ""I Love Marketing" and had attended his marketing Meetup groups in the past. Joe needed someone on his team to support the publishing of his podcast and other marketing tasks. I had the opportunity to work with his team (and I still do).

Joe is a highly skilled marketer and runs a high-level mastermind group for entrepreneurs. It's called the Genius Network. I've had a chance to attend these group discussions with entrepreneurs who run diverse businesses, including one that brings in $9 million in revenue. There's even one billionaire in the group.

This has helped to refine my thinking of how marketing works, which is why I'm sharing it here. I'm going to narrow down what I've learned from attending these events and learning from and meeting people like Tim Ferriss, Daymond John, Arianna Huffington, Mike Koenigs, Darren Hardy, Jeff Walker, Dean Graziosi ... the list goes on and on.

Joe Polish published a podcast episode that was very popular. Its provocative title was "Branding=Bullsh*t?" I found this interesting, because in the past I've done logos and branding for clients. In this case, he was referring to the phenomenon in which people think ""marketing" is the same as building a "brand". That is, marketing by just putting your logo out there, thinking that if people see it 14 times it will compel them to trust you and want to do business with you. That's simply not enough.

After hearing the comments about what people believe branding is or isn't, I was inspired to write a blog post about "the online branding rat race". The more I wrote and talked to clients about it, the more I realized that people do not care about your logo, or your brand.

People don't even care about your company. What do they care about? They care about themselves. About their needs, their problems – and the solutions to their problems.

My good friend Bob Burg, a bestselling author, has been a guest on my podcast a few times. He's an amazing educator on the topic of referral marketing and has written an excellent book titled "It's Not About You".

I learned a lot from Bob's books early in my business career, prior to meeting and getting to know him. I read his books because I respected and valued his perspective on how to get referrals and new business.

Have you ever felt that competing against the corporate giants is just too great a challenge? After all, if you're a dog trainer, it's hard to compete with the "Dog Whisperer". If you're a coach or consultant trying to keep up with the brand recognition and reputation of Brian Tracy, Darren Hardy or any other of these industry legends, it probably feels impossible to catch up.

Every profession includes someone who is considered an industry leader. They simply market their personal name, company or brand identity, and success seems effortless for them.

When you think of the most popular, well-known doctor, you may think of Dr. Oz. He's everywhere. He's become an authority over time.

But why is it such a struggle for us? Because we're playing a "branding" game we don't need to play.

I'm sure Dr. Oz started out just like everyone else – with education and a desire to help people and add value, one person at a time.

Many business owners are over-concerned that their font is exactly correct in every message because they think they're in the same game as major corporations like Nike – where customers see a simple swoosh mark or "Just do it" and know who they are.

Yes, you should have a consistent image and name. But the goal of your marketing efforts should not be to "get your name out there". When gathering new customers via the Internet, you can get much better results by engaging with your target market. This guide will cover how to do exactly that through content marketing – or, specifically, by doing what we'll cover here: blogging.

Small business owners are not in the same game as corporations, yet they often try to play by the same rules. The goal of the small business owner should be to reach new customers and clients, and to set aside the idea of "building awareness".

One of the first things we learn in sales and marketing is that prospective customers must "know, like and trust" you before they will do business with you.

So salespeople go out and meet with 10 to 15 people per week, try to make friends and build awareness for their business. But simply aiming to make friends that know, like and trust you, and the act of building "awareness" without qualifying prospects, can lead to a lot of wasted time.

Your product or service should solve a problem or fill a need for the consumer. It should make their life better in some way. This means they must have a dissatisfaction in their life that needs to be made better. In my opinion, the entry point where you can gain trust with your customers before they buy is the content on your blog.

You blog allows you to provide solutions, ideas, and resources for people. You don't want to talk about your company's features, products and the awards you've won unless it has something to do about helping the reader. Remember: it's not about you.

When Logos Replace Faces

When companies started to grow, they needed a way to leverage their time, to bring in new clients and develop a ""know, like, trust" relationship faster as a way to create familiarity.

So the "brand" is their company name. When one of their reps wore a "branded" shirt, they made it known they were part of the organization and that they were the brand's ambassador. If customers purchased once from this trusted name, they could trust buying from someone else under that same name banner.

I understand that you may have several people in your organization, and that when they are acquiring customers they represent your brand. What I'm suggesting is that a blog can leverage your marketing efforts by having hundreds of people share your message through social media channels.

I was recently at Infusioncon, which is the big conference that Infusionsoft hosts in Phoenix to give training and insights on using their software to improve email marketing funnels. Leadpages.net founder Clay Collins delivered a presentation in which he said his company gets more business leads and customers by hiring a "content creator" rather than a salesperson. Why? Because the content creator can write a great article once, but it might continue to be read, shared and generate customer leads, 24/7.

You can use content creation as a supplement to your marketing to better leverage your time.

Getting Your Name "Out There"

I recently watched a documentary called "Pink Ribbon Inc." In this film, they studied whether the Pink Ribbon campaigns for breast cancer were really making a difference. It made an interesting point about building awareness.

The debate was that people were passionate about the cause, and that everyone knows the pink ribbon means Susan B. Komen and how you can "race for the cure."

People are sincerely racing for family members and friends, hoping to find a cure. However, when you drill down into the numbers, little progress has been made to find that cure. In fact, according to the film, more women get breast cancer today than when the Pink Ribbon movement started.

Awareness? Yes. Branding? Yes. Actually finding a "cure"? Still up for debate...Not to say it's good or bad, it's just an observation.

The goal of every business should be to make money and be profitable. Don't make the mistake of thinking that "nonprofits" are not profitable – they most certainly are, but instead of the profits going back into the corporation, they are used for some purpose. In the case of the Pink Ribbon campaign, awareness is being built. But people might question whether the funds are supporting the foundation or finding a cure for breast cancer. Time will tell.

As I mentioned, I don't know enough about the Pink Ribbon cause to say if I believe they are making a difference or not, but the film was insightful.

I heard another example from Dean Jackson, who is the co-host with Joe Polish on the IloveMarketing.com podcast. Dean is a direct-response marketing consultant for the real estate industry.

He said he asked a group of realtors if they'd like 50 people to receive an envelope bearing their picture and company name so these people could get to ""know them". (This is what's called "getting your name out there".)

Many audience members said they'd like this. Next, Dean asked the realtors if it would be better if someone handed them an envelope containing 50 names, addresses and telephone numbers of target market clients. They all said that would be much better, for obvious reasons. The smart way to leverage content marketing is to use it as a vehicle that enables people to self-identify themselves, as Dean shared in his example.

It's obvious that your branding is your visual image, since your logo, symbol and colors or fonts keep your image consistent and recognizable. Remember, as we have seen, people do business with those whom they know, like and trust. One way you cultivate trust is by being consistent.

Let's say you met someone at a local business networking event who you remember seeing at an expo last week. He said his name was John. The following week, John walks up and tells you his name is George. You think that perhaps this is someone else, but he mentions that they remember meeting you last week. Suddenly, you don't trust John or George.

The same would be true for your business name. If you're starting a new business, going from George Supplies Inc. This month to

Supplier George Inc. The next month would violate people's trust, even if you think it's no big deal.

My point in giving you this example is that the branding is the foundation, but my opinion and experience – which is backed by many other smart marketing professionals – is that you shouldn't market for "branding" alone. Unless, of course, you have a massive budget to throw away and no need to make a return.

This is why I don't recommend using social media marketing to brand your business. You should use it to leverage your efforts to get customers – period.

Along the way, people will recognize your name and start to trust your brand. Branding should happen as a result of getting customers. Branding yourself for the sake of your ego injects no value into the marketplace.

The confusion happens when the term "branding" and "reputation" are used interchangeably. I have heard marketers out there say, "You have to let people know your brand." That makes sense in the context of the message or mission of your business.... however by leading with your "brand" alone you may be missing the mark when communicating your value to the marketplace.

CHAPTER 2

Effective Blogging

M OST PEOPLE ASK, "Do I need to be a great writer to have an effective blog?" The answer is yes and no. I think you do need to have some basic writing skills; however, most blogging platforms including WordPress have spell check features so you don't need to be great at spelling. Grammar is important and so is writing a clear message, but neither is important if your customer feels as though you can help solve a problem for them and they see you as an expert in your field.

Blogging is not about you; it's all about solving the needs and problems of your target audience, so your goal should be just that. I'll cover a few tips if you are writing your own blog and need help in this area.

1. Speak about your topic first: Use a digital recorder or basic voice recording application. Come up with a topic that is a common question amongst your target customer and record yourself answering that question as if they were sitting right in front of you.

2. Bullet Points: Avoid being cliché, but you see this strategy a lot out there because it's effective. You could title a blog, "The 5 things that surprise most first time buyers of [your product category]."

Your outline should consist of three parts: tell them what you are going to tell them, give them the bullet points and explain why each one is important, then summarize and give them a practical tip or action step.

3. Tell A Story: I coach some clients to do an occasional blog post as 'Real World Situation' for you, this could be common errors that you see a client make, don't release their name unless you have their permission. You could explain this as a teaching point for your new clients.

When you are viewed as a resource and someone who adds value even when they are not your client, they will understand that they could potentially benefit even more by becoming your client. Also, people like to feel like an insider or like they are getting a special view of what you do behind the scenes.

Two Styles of Writing

There are basically two styles of blogging in general. We previously covered a few types of blog posts consisting of how to put content together, but this is something to consider in order to keep the attention of your audience. This section will cover the objective of everything you write.

There are basically two styles of blogging, Journal or Solution Finding.

You want your blog to be a solution finding blog. Most people write their business blog as a journal for their business. Blog posts such as announcing what their business awards are this month, new stuff about their company, as well as many other things all about you, when the reader is actually looking for specific personal benefits.

A journal style blog is great if you are planning a wedding or writing about your kids and family as a way of informing distant family of what's going on in your life. However, a business using a journal style blog only causes less clicks and rolling eyes.

Sure, it's nice to blend this into your content, but it should only be about 10% of what you put out. After writing a few blog posts, many people run out of things to brag about regarding their company; no one is reading anyway so they soon give up on creating new articles.

When you create a solution finding blog; everything you write should speak to the needs and wants of your target market, as well as attempt to solve their problems. This brings me to the second challenge most business owners have with their blog; they want to get the attention of "everyone".

When you try to get the attention of everyone, you usually attract no one.

Some people, like me, hesitate on getting too narrow of a target audience because it seems like you might miss out on some potential customers by leaving them out.

Two Doors, Pick One...

While that makes sense, also imagine that you have a Home Builder company. You visit a business expo and there are two booths; one booth has a sign that states, "GG Website Design Services"....well, how attractive is that?

Sounds just like everybody else right?

The second booth has a sign that says, "YC Website Design For Home Builders". I imagine you wouldn't hesitate to walk right in because that booth is serving the needs of people "just like you".

YC creates a recognized name; I see this as branding.

However, the content marketing they do on their blog can be a wealth of value that their target market sees as value and information that is easy to share with other Home Builders.

Let's say they are at the Home Builder association the following day, and they are talking with another home builder who mentions they need a new website. I can imagine the conversation would come up about a Web Design company just for Home Builders. It's specific and it's for them.

What if your company is not that niche specific? You could create specific specials or packages designed for that niche.

The web design company could have a Home Builder Web Package.

When you create a process for a niche you serve, it adds value to you and to what you do. Doctors are well paid, but the highest paid doctors are what?

Specialists.

How Blogging Trumps Branding

Blogging may seem like more work upfront, but it's an online asset that will start working for you if done correctly. Marketing for "awareness" alone results in a poor return on investment in most cases and blogging is turning sweat equity into an online asset that can bring you leverage. By the end of this guide, you'll know how to create a blog that will go to work for you.

Just like my friend Tom Trush mentions in his book, The You Effect, most marketing messages are ego based while the most effective marketing messages are YOU based.

I suppose this is the time you can decide whether you'd like a big ego or a big bank account. My assumption is that marketing fails for many small business owners for that very reason; they are trying to impress everyone with what they have in order to make their ego big.

Having a successful blog means being focused directly on the service and value you can provide to your audience. My friend Bob Burg, who I mentioned earlier, calls it, "The Law Of Value".

The Law Of Value says, "Your true worth is determined how much more you give in value that you take in payment".

Blogging is the best way to provide value up front in a way that can also leverage your time and enhance your marketing.

Blogging helps you to align your value in a way that can leverage your marketing, credibility and reach so you build trust in a way that a faceless corporation cannot.

Jeremy Jones

CHAPTER 3

Your Perfect Blogging Plan

YOU MAY HAVE purchased this book to find your perfect blogging plan and be the first to tell you, any plan or strategy you learn here is not the only plan that works...it's just what I've found to be effective.

I'll tell you the blogging plan that works the best, is the one you actually "work".

So many people seek out new tactics, but very few put it into action.

Building a blog will take planning and work but it's well worth it. My challenge to you would be after you finish this book, simple write down two actions you will take as a result of what you learned here... get out your calendar, and mark down when you will do it.

If you've done that, send me an email and tell me about your plans because I want to support and encourage you for taking action.

Email me at info@AskJeremyJones.com

My greatest hope for you is that you will get started. It doesn't need to be perfect you just have to get started. Really, there is no "perfect" blogging plan...but if there is a plan that you could call perfect it would be the one that you personally could do consistently and enjoy doing along the way. Start with something that is easy to fit into your schedule.

As of this point here are a few actions you can do that would be helpful.

Write out a description of your perfect client, the one you are hoping with read this blog that you want to do business with. Write out a list of the top 3 nagging problems or challenges they deal with on a regular basis. Take each of those major issues, and create 3 questions they may ask you about how to solve it. This list of 9 or 10 things will be your first blog titles.

The blog titles should sound like what the person would type into Google:
How to get rid of…
How to stop….
When is the best time to...

How Often Should You Blog?

In my opinion the best blogging plan is one you can stick to on a regular basis for about 90 days. Then you can re-evaluate how you want to adjust, but a 3 month plan is something anyone can stick to.

You may prefer longer blog posts where you can write out a lot of helpful tips all at once you may only need to post one or two blog posts per month. If you struggle with coming up with content to write or just prefer to write shorter posts, maybe 300-400 words but make it very helpful information with a very attractive headline and I'd recommend posting one per week if you can keep up with that.

There is no perfect answer here, the right answer is how often can you do it and stick with it long enough to check the results.

Shorter posts seem to work well more often and longer posts work fine posting once or twice per month. Any less than one per month and your audience won't know what to expect from you.

If writing a new post every week sounds like a painful activity to you, then you can create a helpful youtube video, create an audio podcast or conduct an interview with helpful information and embed it in your blog post. Write out a couple of bullet points on what they will learn and poof! You're a blogger without having to really write anything.

Systems And Habits

Create a simple strategy in the way you put together a blog post until you get the hang of it. In this guide you'll get lots of ideas that will give you inspiration as to what include for your readers to enjoy and help their life.

Decide how often you'll write a blog post and what day of the week you'll publish it. I normally will write a blog post no more that a few days before it's published. I'm not naturally a writer so it was a real struggle for me in coming up with stuff to write about.

This is part of the reason I've put together this guide to help you avoid the deer in headlights gaze staring at the blinking cursor like I used to do. I wish I would have had a simple guide like this on best practices and a simple plan of action when I got started.

We all have systems of the way we do things. If you have a regular commute we usually drive the same way every day. We have habits that are developed so we have certainty in our lives and as you develop a daily or weekly routine it will get easier and easier to put out great content on your blog.

CHAPTER 4

A Simple Content Creation Plan

MANY FIRST TIME bloggers get overwhelmed coming up with content on a regular basis. Or they write one or two posts that are like mini-novels, spilling their guts about everything they know then the ideas just run dry.

With a simple content creation plan for yourself, you will literally never run out of great ideas to blog about. The economy changes, people change, careers change, rules change, all sorts of things change, so as a result, people's problems and concerns change, and we blog about solving problems. If you use the strategy laid out for you in this guide, you can always come back as a reminder of the best content to use in a blog.

One tool I really enjoy using is Evernote. It's a web application that can sync to a mobile application for taking notes, typed and audio. You can take notes or take pictures. Evernote also lets you add tags to each note, so you can easily find what you need.

If you have ideas, just jot them down and add the tag "Blog" or whatever you choose to use for your ideas. When you sit down to write your blog post, open Evernote, click the tag "Blog", and all your thoughts, ideas and notes from the week will be there, and you'll have plenty of ideas to choose from.

During your week find a time you can set aside 30 minutes to write your blog post, if you are using wordpress you can schedule your post to publish in 24 hours and this will give you time to give it one last review or search for a great picture or two to include in your post. Give yourself time to get into the habit of blogging on a regular basis and as you'll learn later it will turn many of your marketing efforts that have produced little results into an online asset for you that makes social media fun and engaging with the content you publish.

Keep in mind, these don't need to be long writings...it's more important you get into the habit, than the quality of the content itself. The quality will improve, and as long as you are focused on the topic of the needs and challenges of your ideal reader, you'll be fine.

How to Come Up With Content That Readers Crave

What if you created content on your blog that people craved? What if they hungered for your content like a bloodhound searching for food? Let's cover a few tips on how you can get your readers to appreciate your every crumb like a feast and not every feast you prepared like a crumby meal.

This is an interesting discussion here, because we assume we know exactly what our customers want. They want to stumble across your website and in most cases do not purchase on the first visit.

This will be a story to give an illustration of the concept of coming up with attractive content. Because I don't know who your target reader is, it's hard for me to tell you what to write, but I'll give you a story of why you are writing and show you how to find hungry readers.

Here's a story to illustrate. Imagine a hunter goes out with his trusty bloodhound to shoot a duck out in the marshes right at the peak of duck season. He's been excited about this trip for a while, goes out, and immediately sees the perfect pheasant. He takes a shot and nails it, and it rapidly drops directly to the ground.

The hunter cues his bloodhound to go bring it back proudly. Now, imagine you're the bloodhound. You dart into the marsh, racing out there as quickly as possible, you catch a scent of something, sniff around, and realize it's a rabbit...not to get sidetracked, you quickly dart in another direction.

Too many scents, too little time. The incredible smelling ability of the bloodhound picks up all kinds of scents, but doesn't get distracted until finally, below his nose, is the duck. The dog quickly grabs it up and brings it to his owner to share the news and proudly get a pat on the back.

What does this mean for you? Well, I think the bloodhound searching is what people do when they search online. It has been said that people go online and surf around, searching for information to solve a problem more than anything else.

The problem is to find the duck. The distractions are all the other websites that either smell like a solution to your customer's problem or just might take them on the wrong trail. Many people do this. I do, and I'm sure you can relate. You look for an answer to something, google the answer, scan the first few results, click a website, scan it, and if I don't see what I'm looking for, I quickly jump back to google and check out some other results.

You're creating the bait your clients want. What content, or bait, can you put out that is attractive and compelling for them?

A blog, when done correctly, provides answers to your customers' problems, answers questions about their needs, wants, don't wants and frequently asked questions. If they like the answer, they might share it on their social network channels.

Do you know who shares sales pages on Social Media? Only the guy that owns the sales page.

CHAPTER 5

Getting People To Share Your Blog

NOW THAT YOU have an understanding of what attracts readers, and it's all about them and their interests, let's discuss what causes them to, not only read, comment or click Like, but also share your blog post.

The first thing to keep in mind is to make it easy for them. If they have to search around on the page for the social share buttons, that's too much work. If they have to copy and paste the URL of your blog post, then go over to Facebook and share, forget about it...that is grueling labor for your readers. I'm only half kidding.

As I stated in the last section, people will not share a sales message, but they will share useful information or something that's entertaining. This is why the LOL cats on Facebook have 3800 shares, and your town hall award announcement for your groundbreaking research is struggling to get 3 Likes.

Keep in mind, people are always asking themselves, "what does this have to do with ME??

We'll never beat the LOL cats, probably, and I'm shocked, as I'm sure you are as well, they even came up here, but we can also create content that is share worthy and meaningful at the same time.

How do the LOL cats make people's lives better? Entertainment.

Three Types of Content We Love Sharing

1. How-to guides

Tell stories, give instructions, and teach some concepts that give people a little something interesting to think about during the day. That's fun to share.

2. Infographics

When putting together stats or interesting figures, people love visuals. Tell interesting facts and relate with people and connect with them in situations they deal with every day. If you are going to compare percentages, use a pie chart. Also, comparing sizes shows two relative objects in size like a pickup truck and a semi-truck shown as silhouette illustrations, comparing their size. This contrast of two objects gives us a visual, and readers like it.

3. A List of Things [like this one you are reading]

Sometimes, we just scan the blog post, and when we see an outline or a bullet point list, we stop and look at each point. We like the list; we share the list. We don't want to type out the list ourselves; it's easier to just click "share", because you already did the work for them.

You see I'm giving you tons of value by outlining 3 different things you can do that people already share freely with their social networks. Use this as a regular resource guide in your blogging efforts and review this guide once a month for your 90 day blogging plan.

You can add value to your readers by doing a bullet point list.

The key to making sharing work for you is two parts. One being the headline and two being the first paragraph. When your post is shared on social networks, this is what everyone else sees. Now you have a chance to compel someone new to click and learn more. When you stretch beyond your reach and attract people beyond your own social network, your blog is like a full-time marketing soldier, going out into battle while you are awake or sleeping.

How awesome is that?

We are looking for your blog to help you create leverage in your marketing. We want your blog to be working for you as an online asset day and night, so we are not marketing online all the time, but we're spending time with our family.

Gain access to free exclusive book bonus training on how to gain massive exposure of your content marketing in as little as 15 minutes per day. On your cell phone text CLIENTBAIT to phone number 33444

Jeremy Jones

CHAPTER 6

Engaging Your Readers

THE BEST AND most effective blogs have the most engagement. They have a community of regular readers who comment and connect. The author of the blog post should closely monitor comments and reply to every comment. If you comment on a blog several times and get no reply, it's not likely you'll continue commenting.

Comments are the starting point of engagement on your blog. This creates a dynamic community environment that a static website has no competition against. It gives you an unfair advantage.

Increasing Your Levels of Engagement

The lowest level of engagement on your blog is someone clicking Like or +1. This means they like the post, appreciate what you're sharing, but it's not worth the trouble to comment or share.

The next level in engagement with your readers is when they share your post with their social networks. They feel like this would be of value to their connections, and they are proud to associate their profile with your blog.

Another level in engagement is commenting on your blog; it comes in close second, but I elevated it to the next level because they have to put down their thoughts and usually sign in with their email if they are not already. Their comment is permanently tied to this blog post, and other people will see their reply.

One level higher would be if they tag you in a post in response to your ideas or respond to a question you prompted in your blog post. It's also very good to see readers responding and connecting with other readers. Allow people to freely communicate and express their feedback and opinions, positive or negative. It's ok to disagree or allow other people to disagree, as long as everyone is polite to each other. If I get someone who is negative, critical, or rude, who has joined my email list and follows my blog, I will often invite them to unsubscribe. I don't care about having the biggest community, but I do want quality.

Gaining More Subscribers

There are basically two common ways for people to subscribe to your new blog posts. One is RSS, Really Simple Syndication, which means you can have new blog posts from 100 blogs all feed into one reader, and so you don't have to visit 100 websites.

My favorite RSS reader is Feedly.com; it's awesome and easy to use. Feedly.com lets you organize your feeds into folders very easily. My favorite way is to scan my RSS feeds on my mobile phone with Feedly as a way to look at new blog posts and podcasts I follow. It's an incredibly innovative app, and once I started using it, my life was never the same. I'm only half kidding. It did save me some time though.

The second way to build subscribers is by collecting emails. You can do this with a subscribe form on your blog, and it's managed by email marketing software, such as Aweber or Mailchimp. It works well to put together a give-away, such as a free report, eBook, or free mp3 audio. You offer to give them something they want for something you want, which is permission to communicate with them by email.

This is one important reason we covered your ideal customer in the first section. Take the answers you wrote down as to your target markets' most burning question. Put together something exclusive that will compel people to want to get your free give-away, and at the same time, permission to subscribe them to your blog updates.

This is also helpful when you write articles or guest post on other blogs. You can mention that, not only do you blog on [mention your website] that helps people [2 or 3 benefits], but stop by to get a free eBook that shows people how to avoid [what they don't want] and get more of [what they want more than anything else]. Fill in the blanks from your answers to your target market, and you'll have an irresistible offer your target market can't refuse.

Your Unfair Advantage Offline

Do you want to have a fair shot, equal chance, among everyone out there? Of course not, we all want an unfair advantage, and with a blog, you can give yourself an unfair advantage online and offline. Major companies have an unfair advantage against you with multi-million dollar ad campaign budgets just for "name recognition" or branding. I'm going to show you, by following a simple blogging roadmap, where you can have an unfair advantage and how to get started.

You'll learn how to gain an unfair advantage online and offline in a way that is so simple you can apply it right way.

How to use a blog offline

Some people may argue blogging is just for techies, and I'm not much of an online marketing person. Here are a few creative ideas you can use on your blog online or offline.

Well, if you want, mail postcards with value added tips to every one of your customers and prospective customers with the hopes they get so excited about your tips they throw a pile of postcards in the area, and the wind blows them into the neighborhood yards, which is free trashy advertising for you. Be my guest. Social Networking sites are a way to leverage word of mouth; you just need to give them a reason to spread the word.

I do think postcards have their place and are actually a great way to market now that very few do it. Also, business cards are great in networking event situations as well, but I'll explain why blogging can benefit you offline, and I think you'll be pleasantly surprised about the creative ideas you can come up with.

Real Life Example

Let's say you're a business trainer, and you do presentations to help sales reps acquire more customers. When you attend a networking event, you could mention you're a speaker and sales trainer; it's short and very clear what you do. But who do you know that needs a sales trainer? I have no idea

They ask me, do I know of anyone that would benefit from a sales trainer, and I draw a blank...what about you?

Let's try a different approach. You meet someone at a networking event, they ask what you do for a living, and you reply with a response like, "You know there are a lot of companies struggling to get ahead right now?", and the reply might be, "Yeah, it does seem like there are."

Your reply could be, as an example, "Well, I help those companies that have sales teams that could use further training, so they make more money for the company."

Like magic, they reply, "You know, in fact, I do…I know a guy at a security company where they have sales people."

You reply with value up front, not "Oh wow, can you give me that referral so I can make a cold call."

You respond by saying, "Well, I wrote a blog post recently that covers the 5 bad habits sales teams develop and how to correct them. If I email you a link to that blog post, would you mind passing it along to your friend, and also ask if he could pass it along to the sales manager. Maybe it would help."

Value Driven Marketing Wins

Wow, isn't that a more professional way to market a business with offering value first? Who does this? Very few, but I'll be the first to tell you, I personally do, and it's created a nice stream of referrals, customers, and new blog subscribers.

By the way, do we want a good fair, even playing field? Nope, this is free enterprise. If you work harder and put more value in the marketplace, you absolutely should be compensated greater.

In fact, you could have a new blog post every month and target different referral sources every month from the same networking events or lead exchange groups you attend.

Your Unfair Advantage

Now, I'm sure it's clear to you this advantage you'd have, especially among your peers and competition. Most people are so eager to just get a customer for their needs alone, they work the hard path that appears to be the easy path. If you could create an army of people, sharing your message via your blog day and night, whether or not you are awake and actively promoting your business, that's leverage.

Looking Back On Branding

Going back to the "branding" issue, I'm not saying your business should not be branded. You should have a consistent name, message, and image. People becoming familiar with your message is branding you. This is coming from someone who has a graphic arts background, also….remember, I realize the image of your business is important; however, your marketing efforts should not have an objective to do "branding." They should be to get you clients and customers for life, and a side benefit is you become a recognized brand by familiarity.

CHAPTER 7

Social Media Syndication Domination

U SING SOCIAL MEDIA strategy in your business marketing plan should be a way to add value to your followers and be a resource to those that choose to like your personal or business social media pages.

You should be less like music artists, who play all their own music on the loud speaker and more like a DJ. An online DJ shares music the audience wants to hear. Based on topics your audience is interested in, you can share and promote other people and ideas, most of the time, and after you give enough value, only then you can promote yourself. The person who promotes only their own contest can make an audience grow weary.

What Is The Objective Of Using Social Media?

So, really, the goal is to create know, like, trust relationships. If you have a company name with a very simple logo and a one page website that includes a blog, you are finished branding your company. I see so many "social media gurus" that say you need to build awareness or brand your business on Twitter or Facebook. That's great, but people don't care about your company name or logo. They want to solve a problem in their life or have a way to make their life better.

If you strive for pursuing your marketing efforts for branding yourself alone, you'll end up always being the hunter for customers. You should aim to get customers by promoting value first, the branding will come along the way.

After all, would you rather be known as the person with the orange logo or the person that is looking to add value first?

I think this one of the things small business owners or someone starting a home business, where they are self-employed, face a challenge. They simply don't have a budget, in most cases, to pay for branding, and frankly there is no need. You or your graphic designer can create a consistent look that can be used in your marketing. After that, your efforts are to create an end result of getting more customers.

Challenge of marketing online

We are living in a time with overwhelming numbers of advertisements being pushed at us. You wake up and see ads, drive to work and see billboards, and hop on Facebook to see floods of ads all over; everyone is trying to grab your attention any way they can to interrupt us.

If you personally get annoyed with all the ads, companies shouting about how their product is the best, you can't live without it and you should buy it, regardless if they know your need or not, then what happens when you do the same thing on social networking? You appear to your network, just like everyone else.

This strategy works, obviously. A small percentage of the people will have a need at that time, and it's extremely expensive. It's just not practical for self-employed or small business owners with a low marketing budget.

These companies are trying to "brand" their company with the hopes that a fraction of a fraction will respond the campaign. If you don't have $15,000 per month to put into ads to get your "name out there", then I'd encourage you to be open to a better way.

I'd suggest blogging is that better way. Blogging can allow you to develop market research from your audience based on what they respond or reply to. Create compelling headlines based on the exact needs of your target market in a way that attracts them then compels them to take a specific action.

When they like the value you add on your blog, they share your content with their social networks.

Here is where the real leverage comes in. If you have 200 friends on Facebook, and let's say 4 of them like your message and click "like", assuming each has around 100 friends, you'd get your message potentially seen by 400 brand new people. However, with Facebook's recent changes, only a small fraction will actually view it, so your first exposure to those people will be of greater benefit to those people by offering a useful blog post, rather than a dull company website. That's better "branding" by getting your value to "brand" new people.

When you shout from the rooftops about how great your company is, you look like everybody else. When someone else recommends, likes, or shares your message, especially with a positive comment added, it carries at least 20 times the weight.

Think of it this way; if you ran into a guy, asked what he did, and he told you, "I'm a dentist" - you reply, "Oh really, it's your own office?" He responds by saying, "Yep, we're the best dentist office in the valley. We've been around for 5 years," and goes on bragging and telling you how you have GOT to come by and get a cleaning! That carries a certain amount of weight. Of course, he thinks he's the best, just like everyone else. After all, he's probably trying to just make money off me. That's the normal response for most people.

However, you run into some, and they say, "I just left the dentist office." You reply by saying, "Oh that reminds me; I need to make an appointment. How are they over there?" When they reply they've been going there for 5 years, everyone is friendly, and it's a great experience, it's exactly that; the recommendation is a different experience.

My point is a blog is an online asset you develop where you market with all value up front. Your content should speak directly to the needs, wants, don't wants, problems and common concerns, and questions of your target market. You can title your blog posts by asking common questions people ask you.

Getting Blog Traffic from Social Media

If you were due for a dentist appointment and someone shared a post on Facebook or Twitter with the headline, "How to completely avoid visiting the dentist," If you're like me, even out of pure curiosity, I'd stop by and read it; and if it was clear, brief and educational, they would position themselves as someone who wanted to help me first.

Let's say the article explained how to care for your teeth, but however, we recommend you get two cleanings per year. Fill out this quick form to request your appointment, and an additional question, asking openly, what's your #1 concern with dental care? They may get some great feedback or discover a need of this customer.

Why don't more small business owners and self-employed professionals do this? It takes work, and more importantly, it's for abundant minded people.

Why do I say that? The reason is because, some people would say, I don't want them to care for their teeth…the bad news of a cavity is good news for me! Well, we are solution providers. Yes, I would agree, but we develop long-term customers by looking after their needs first.

Wouldn't you rather have 5 people with a positive experience that visit the dentist twice a year, rather than 20 that dread visiting the dentist every time and tell everyone how terrible it is?

After all, the 5 that feel the business is on their side will gladly recommend to everyone they talk to if it comes up in conversation. I had a conversation with my good friend, Ron Broussard, who is a life coach, and he brought up a great point, which I believe in 100 percent; people do business with those they know, like and trust, but also the people they feel a connection with.

Blogging effectively is the best way I know to position yourself as an expert and connect with your target markets needs and wants; the only thing better would be a one on one conversation, and that could easily transition into your next step.

Jeremy Jones

CHAPTER 8

That Very Few Do

W E HAVE COVERED 7 different areas that will help you develop an unfair advantage and crush the competition by building your "client bait."

Keep in mind the fishing analogy. In order to catch the fish you want, you have to do two things: Use the bait the fish want (blog post that delivers value to them) and have your fishing line in the water (taking action).

Also, as you take action, you'll want to follow this 80 / 20 rule. Spend 20% of your time writing the blog post and spend 80% of the time you have set aside for content creation to promote your blog post. Pro-actively share the articles you create.

I'm going to encourage you to give yourself a full, unfair advantage by putting each of the 7 parts into action and send us your results. Maybe you can be the next success story we feature on our blog or next coaching product. A few of the steps were mindset, or a perspective change, as to how you think about content creation or content marketing.

A Blogging Blueprint

Have you attempted to start blogging, but didn't know where to start? Maybe you wrote a few posts, then you just ran out of things to talk about. I'd like to share why blogging is challenging for most people and what to do about it.

Now you know the 7 parts and you need to take action. They say that knowledge is power, but I disagree. Applied knowledge is power; the application of the 7 steps gives you an unfair advantage, because it's not natural to give first. Many people want to sell first.

It's pretty simple to create a blog. But what do you do next?

Now, we will cover why, I believe, most people blog once or twice then leave their blog to collect dust on a small tab off to the side of their website.

If you are doing that, you are leaving money on the table. It's like having money in a checking account but not having a debit card to access it.

A correctly used blog can literally be an asset you develop online, and if you make Blogging part of your marketing, identifying who your ideal reader is, and then creating the content bait, and putting your lines in the water, you'll see your blog come alive with engagement, interaction, and a growing audience.

A Simple 7 Step Blogging Blueprint after You Publish

It helps to break down a big idea, like online marketing, into a few simple parts. Now that you know the 7 part plan to turn your blog into client bait that attracts your ideal customers and grow your audience, you're ready for a basic outline to keep in mind as you get started.

Remember the 8th step is take action. It's not enough to just know what to do. It's putting a plan into place, taking action, checking the results, and adjusting where you learn what will work best for your blog. The great thing about blogging is you can test things pretty easily, add new landing pages, or make new offers to see what grabs people's attention.

If you keep these 3 Steps in mind, all of your online marketing efforts will be more effective.

Expose. Engage. Upgrade.

Expose

First, list all of the ways you can expose your blog to new people on a regular basis. You may plan to bring it up in conversation more often, add it to your email signature, share new blog posts with attention grabbing headlines on your social media channels, and more.

There are lots of ways to expose your blog to more people. Start with 2-3 that you feel would be the lowest hanging fruit, meaning, simple, cost effective ways you can get more exposure to your blog on a regular basis and go for it.

Twitter can be a powerful tool for getting your blog exposure. If you are familiar with Twitter, it's an open conversation platform. Be sure to use #Hashtags when you share your links related to topics and trending topics so your Tweets can get found.

When you Tweet with a #Hashtag, such as #Blogging or #BloggingTips, you can click on the #hashtag, and it will search for everyone else who has tweeted that same hashtag.

Each social network has its pros and cons, and not to bash Facebook, but the reality is that if you have a business page with 10,000 likes, and you post an update, only 10 to 20% will even see your post, unless you pay for a promoted status update. You did all the hard work to build those fans, but you can't freely engage with them. This alone is why I have put the majority of my business efforts into using Twitter as my hub, and the others come secondary.

Expose, Engage

Find several ways you can engage with your readers. The first would be, most importantly, to reply to every single comment on your blog. Thank people, reply to comments, ask for feedback, and look for ways to add value to your readers.

We covered the various levels of engagement on a blog. You should be engaging with people inside and outside your blog. One great way to share your blog, and how I was able to grow my followers from a few hundred to over 10,000 on Twitter, is by sharing quality content and retweeting (sharing) content from my followers also.

In each of the social platforms, you can find places where your target market gathers, based on their interests. LinkedIn has affinity groups, Facebook has groups (some private some public), Twitter has Twitter Chats using #hashtags, and Google Plus has communities.

I'm sure to add value to a community, first, by sharing interesting or funny things I find then commenting and connecting with others. If I have a blog post I feel would help the members of the community or I think they might find useful, I share it there. I enjoy engaging with people within groups, and it's a great way to develop solid relationships with other people, who will also share your blog posts with their network.

Another great way to engage with new people, who may have an interest in your new blog posts on Twitter or Google+, is by using hashtags. As an example, if you see a post with #SXSW and you click, it will bring up a search page where you can see everyone else who has posted that same hashtag related to the South by Southwest Event, which uses #SXSW for Tweets related to that community. You can then engage and start a conversation about it.

Anyone else who searches that tag will see your post. More Exposure. As you have learned here, exposure is good, but it's not enough, standing alone. Your blog is the catalyst that can move people along from expose, to engage, to upgrade.

When someone else shares your post, they create engagement with their network and you get more of step one, exposure. See, when you share your own post, its promotion. When someone else shares it, then it's pure value. Always thank people and show appreciation for others. I have a group where content creators can connect, guest post for each other, and share each other's content.

If you want an invite to one of those groups, send me an email to: info@AskJeremyJones.com

1. Expose, 2. Engage, 3. Upgrade

Let's go back to my point that we are not doing all this just to "build awareness", our goal is to add value to others and help improve some area of their life with our product, services, or business. You can't really improve someone's life just by writing a status update or even a blog post. It's just a starting point.

The way you set yourself apart and gain an unfair advantage in your marketing is by adding value first, giving out your best education, and solution providing for free. Some may question this strategy that people will just take the information and run, but it's quite the opposite. A real live example would be to recall if you have ever been to a food court when they offer a free sample of food on the toothpick.

You can only take the free sample so many times before you feel guilty and go buy yourself a meal. When you upgrade your audience, they are elevating their level of commitment, first, by time, invested in reading, and next, the commitment of exchanging their email, giving you permission to communication. When they see you are "safe" and are not going to spam bomb them, they begin to trust you.

Trying to only sell from social media is jumping directly to "Upgrade." It's like asking someone to marry you the first time you meet them...it's creepy, and in their eyes, happening way too fast.

Why would anyone hand you money online before having enough trust to offer their email?

They quicker you build trust, the faster they will get upgraded to a paying customer. Give enough upfront, they may just feel "obligated" to buy. However, this is not the objective. When you have something that will solve the problem of another person, it's your moral obligation to offer a solution. People will not only see value in your expertise and want to upgrade to your customer or client, but they may think, "If they give so much great info like this away for free, imagine how I could benefit if I paid for it."

Your first step of upgrade should be low resistance and allow you to communicate directly with them. Seth Godin wrote a great book, called "Permission Marketing", where he explains the idea of email marketing and gaining permission to receive a marketing message. His book was really cutting edge at the time when this was a new concept. At the time I am writing this, collecting an email from a website is common practice; however, I hope the expose, engage, upgrade model will help you build a framework, so you can apply this is in your marketing efforts on your blog.

When and Where To Share

Now that your blog marketing plan is starting to form, a lot of common questions I get are that you may be confused with all the social media platforms out there. After all, you're already posting on Facebook, Google+, maybe Twitter, trying to figure out how to use Instagram for your business, and even more confused how to use Vine...you may think adding a blog writing plan would be very time consuming.

I'm going to suggest using one or two platforms where you feel your target audience is most likely to be and where you have the most potential. If you see the potential of Twitter for sharing your blog content, like I do, then lay out a basic plan as to how you'll share your blog posts there.

Here is a basic syndication plan I use that is simple and doesn't take a lot of time.

It starts with Twitter as my hub. So if you are not on Twitter yet or chose to use another one, it is perfectly fine.

I like Twitter, because when you share a Tweet, the stream of content people get can be fast; however, it's not filtered, like Facebook. If they are on Twitter at that time, they more than likely will see it. Then you add appropriate #hashtags to help extend the life of what you Tweet.

Remember Expose, Engage, and Upgrade are our key profit activators for turning blogging into profits, so any time you can get more of either of these three, you'll be in good shape.

Here are my suggestions. Adjust it as you see appropriate:

Write a blog post with a compelling headline
Publish it.
Search Twitter for "trending topics." See if any apply to your post. If so, note the #hashtags
Post an interesting image, link to your blog, and include 1-3 #tags.
If you mention anyone in your blog post, +tag them. They may share your post.
Share your own post in an appropriate groups and include a question to start engagement.
On your blog post, share with all your social networks [social buttons plugin].
Find a way to relate it to your blog post. Tweet with #tags.
Check Facebook groups related to topic of your blog post.
Facebook Group: Post a link to your blog post and include a question to start engagement.

Social networks create exposure, your engagement influences others to share the value you put out, and this creates more exposure and gives you leverage in your marketing.

You, alone, promote. It's all on your efforts. You use your blog post to add value to others by your content, and when they share your blog with their network, it adds value to them and creates more exposure for you. Don't track your website just by "hits." Website or blog hits don't mean anything; the conversion of exposures and your process in how you upgrade them to offer them more value is what you look for.

Cross-Promotional Partners

Developing relationships with other bloggers is a way to create win-win engagement and more exposure at the same time. One of the most important things you can do, as a self-employed professional or small business owner, is develop win-win relationships with other business owners. You would be surprised how with people, who seem to be your competition, you can develop some sort of cross-promotional partnership.

This all starts with cultivating relationships and connecting with other people.

As I mentioned earlier in this book, if you only promote yourself, people become weary of your message and stop paying attention. You can add value to your followers on your social networks, like being a DJ, by spinning out great content you find or interesting, funny or inspiring bits of content. You can share random things you come across, or you can develop a list of people who you pro-actively keep an eye on their blog and share what you find useful.

A cross-promotional partner would be someone who agrees to share your posts with their network, and you agree to do the same. Keep in mind one thing. You want to be sure the post is filled with value and quality, and you feel it may be of interest to your network.

Your blog posts will carry more weight when someone else calls you an expert and suggests your blog more often than you shouting from the rooftops how the gems you just published will change lives and inspire the world.

Self-promotion causes blank stares and rolling eyes…if your ratio of value and self-promotion is off. Yes, you need both, and there is no exact formula, but Gary Vaynerchuk is the expert in using social media tools for marketing. In his book, titled "Jab, Jab, Jab, Right Hook", he uses a boxing analogy that you want to jab with value and engagement many times before you ask for anything from them.

Many new entrepreneurs are familiar with the cliché, "kill the competition." Big thinkers and the most successful entrepreneurs don't think this way. They think abundantly and worry very little about the competition as a threat. They network with other business owners and look for ways to benefit everyone involved.

Before you can collaborate with someone, you first have to connect.

Guest Posting

One very effective way to get more new visitors to your blog is by writing short blog posts that are displayed on another blog with a similar target audience. At the end of your blog, it will include an author box, where you have a link back to your website. Do a search on Google for your key term or phrase that you write about on your blog. In the search options, select "blogs." This will do a search, indexing only blogs. You can reach out to the blog owners, leave a comment, and compliment them first, and get to know them. When the time is right, offer to contribute a guest blog post.

Accept Guest Posts

It's important to not only put out guest posts, but one very effective strategy in getting others to share your blog is to feature someone else. Some of my highest unique visitor spikes in traffic have been when I have someone contribute an article on my blog, they can then share it on social media and position themselves as an expert by being featured on another website other than their own.

Track and Improve

After you have your Expose, Engage, Upgrade system moving in the right direction you can start to track your conversion. You should have some sort of a way to capture email addresses by offering something of value to the reader. If your conversion is low start taking surveys or asking those that comment on their common struggles, questions or problems. This is very valuable information that can be used to put together a free ebook, report or video that you can offer in exchange for someone subscribing to your email list.

My friend Joe Polish has told me one tip that is very important and can help you also.

That which you track improves and that which you track and report/get accountability on improves exponentially.

That's the simple 7 steps to do as you work your blogging plan. Expose, Engage and Upgrade should be 3 focus areas. Develop cross promotional partners, guest post, accept guest posts and track and improve your results. Remember to keep things simple and find a good rhythm for your best blogging plan.

Where To Go Next?

Gain access to free exclusive book bonus training on how to gain massive exposure of your content marketing in as little as 15 minutes per day. On your cell phone text CLIENTBAIT to phone number 33444

I want to thank you sincerely for reading this book.

I would greatly appreciate your positive feedback on the Kindle Book page.

Be sure to connect with me on Twitter, @jonesima

Send me an email to let me know you finished this book and what your next 2 actions are as a result of what you learned: info@ AskJeremyJones.com

Subscribe to the blog for free training and articles: AskJeremyJones.com

ABOUT THE AUTHOR

Jeremy Jones is a proud Military veteran who served in Operation Enduring Freedom, family man, entrepreneur now living in Paradise Valley, Arizona. He started as a freelance professional graphics and multimedia designer after achieving a bachelors of Arts with honors from the Art Institute of Phoenix.

A few years ago he started a podcast to help promote authors, speakers and coaches and help them gain a bigger reach about their book or programs.

He founded Jones Media Publishing as a way to help bring a traditional publishing house level of quality for books to self-publishing and help busy entrepreneurs with ideas or concepts for books and efficiently author their ideas.

Jeremy C. Jones
info@AskJeremyJones.com
@jonesima

Jeremy Jones

www.ingramcontent.com/pod-product-compliance
Lightning Source LLC
Chambersburg PA
CBHW080248200526
45166CB00021B/1311